Maybe I will not be a vet.
What else can I do?

3

I want to fix hair when I grow up.

I will try it once.

# When I Grow Up

Written by Jan Burchett and Sara Vogler

Illustrated by Carol Thompson

Harcourt
Supplemental Publishers

Rigby • Steck-Vaughn

www.steck-vaughn.com

I want to be a vet when I grow up.

I will try it once.

Maybe I will not fix hair.
What else can I do?

I want to be a firefighter when I grow up.
I will try it once.

Maybe I will not be a firefighter.
What else can I do?

I want to grow some plants when I grow up.
I will try it once.

Maybe I will not grow plants.
What else can I do?

I want to build some things when I grow up.

I will try it once.

Maybe I will not build things.

Maybe I will not grow up yet!